The AmJobs Motto:

"Working together...we can fix the Unemployment Problem in America"

AmJobs

(The American Jobs Program)

February 1, 2014

Mission Statement:

The Goal of AmJobs (The American Jobs Program) is to reduce Unemployment in America … by putting Unemployed Americans "back to work"… and upgrade their "Jobs Skills" too.

AmJobs will do this by:

- ❖ <u>**Providing Incentives to "Businesses"**</u>**… that will motivate them to join AmJobs and hire Millions of Unemployed Workers each year.**

- ❖ <u>**Providing incentives to "Unemployed Workers"**</u>**… that will motivate them to join AmJobs and accept a new Temporary Job this year.**

- ❖ <u>**Ensuring that AmJobs is "100% Revenue Neutral"**</u>**… it will not cost the American Taxpayer "one dime"!**

AmJobs Contact Information:

Rocky Lynn, Founder

Email:	*RockyLynn@AmJobs.org*
On-line:	*AmJobs.org (click: "contact us")*
Via Mail:	*AmJobs*
	PO Box 6178
	Jensen Beach, Florida 34957

Letter from the Founder:

Dear Political Leader, Business Leader, and fellow Citizen:

Everyone is concerned about the "Unemployment Problem" in America…and we all want to help put "Unemployed Americans" back to work!

<u>AmJobs</u> (The American Jobs Program) is the innovative new "Job Creation Program" that will <u>Fix</u> our Unemployment Problem fast!

> *<u>Note:</u> I don't want any salary or profit from my AmJobs idea. I just want to encourage Political and Business Leaders to join together…to help create Millions of "New Jobs" and "Training Programs" for Unemployed Workers.*

The purpose of this "Booklet" is to explain the AmJobs Program in detail … and encourage you to join our growing list of Sponsors and Supporters. If you like what you read (or need more information) please contact me.

Sincerely,

Rocky Lynn

Rocky Lynn
AmJobs Founder

<u>Contact Information:</u>
         Via Email: RockyLynn@AmJobs.org
         On-line at: AmJobs.org (click: "contact us")

AmJobs has Six major Goals

1. Motivate Businesses to start hiring again.

2. Create <u>Millions</u> of New Jobs for Unemployed Workers.

3. Provide "Job Skills Training" for <u>Millions</u> of Workers.

4. Help America get back to "Full Employment" in 2 years.

5. Help strengthen our Economy.

6. Ensure that AmJobs pays for itself…and that AmJobs is:

   - 100% "Revenue Neutral".
   - Will <u>not</u> cost the taxpayer "one dime"!

AmJobs Overview
(Next 6 pages)

The next six pages will give a high level "Overview" of the AmJobs Program.

AmJobs Overview

❖ We have a difficult Unemployment Problem in America.

Unfortunately there were 11.5 Million Unemployed Workers in Mid-2013. Many Economists believe that Businesses have over $2 Trillion in cash (on the sidelines) but they are <u>not</u> "Hiring" due to economic uncertainty. What America needs now is a new "Jobs Program" that will motivate Businesses to start hiring again.

❖ What is AmJobs?

AmJobs is the "innovative" new Jobs Program…that will <u>Fix</u> the Unemployment Problem in America…Fast!

❖ What exactly will AmJobs do?

1. Provide "Incentives" to Businesses…that will motivate them to Join AmJobs, and hire 2.9 Million (or more) new Temporary Employees every year.

2. Provide "Incentives" to 2.9 Million "Unemployed Workers"…that will motivate them to Join AmJobs, and accept a new Temporary Job this year.

3. Help America get back to "Full Employment" (4% range) in just two years.

4. Inject $60 Billion of Revenue into our Economy each year.

5. Insure that AmJobs is "100% Revenue Neutral"…and will Pay for itself every year, without any Government Appropriations needed.

Overview (Continued)

❖ What "Incentives" are offered to Businesses and Workers?

■ Incentives to Businesses:

a. AmJobs allows Businesses to "Save up to 40%" on Labor Costs… for new Temporary Employees that they hire through the AmJobs Program.

b. This "40% Labor Savings" will <u>motivate</u> Businesses to join AmJobs…and:
    - ✓ Launch "shovel ready projects"…
    - ✓ Test new Products and Services …
    - ✓ Expand their Businesses …
    - ✓ Hire 2.9 Million Temporary Workers each year.

■ Incentives to Unemployed Workers:

a. AmJobs gives Unemployed Workers "<u>Three</u> <u>Financial Benefits</u>"… which will motivate 2.9 Million of them to Join AmJobs yearly… and accept a new Job. These Benefits are:
    - ■ Keep their "unemployment checks" ($300 value).
    - ■ Receive an additional "Weekly Stipend" ($300 value).
    - ■ Receive weekly "Training Vouchers" ($60 value).

b. Value of Worker Incentives:

Value of Worker Incentives:	Week	Month	Year
- Keep Unemploy. Checks:	$300	$1300	$15,600
- Worker "Stipends":	$300	$1300	$15,600
- "Training Vouchers":	$ 60	$ 260	$ 3,120
- Total Benefits:	$660	$2860	$34,320

Overview (Continued)

❖ **How does AmJobs Work?**

➢ **AmJobs Operates using "Two important Mechanisms":**

1. A simple 2-Step "Flow of Funds" Process:

    a. <u>Businesses</u> will pay a weekly "Labor Fee" to the State AmJobs Office. This "Labor Fee" will be equal to 60% of the "normal" hourly wage for each Temporary Employee they hire (<u>Saving them 40% on Labor Expense</u>).

    b. <u>The State AmJobs Office</u> will use this 60% "Labor Fee" (think "Revenue Stream") to pay for all AmJobs <u>Expenses</u>…including:

- Weekly "Stipend Payments" to Workers.
- Weekly "Training Vouchers" to Workers.
- A contribution to each State's "Employment and Training Fund" (explained later).
- All "Operating costs" needed to run AmJobs.

2. A comprehensive "Employment Website… allowing:

    a. <u>Businesses</u> to enter: Job postings, new-hire information, and calculate their weekly "60% Labor Fees" (to be sent to the State AmJobs Office).

    b. <u>State AmJobs Offices</u> to allocate Revenue (60% Labor Fees) to pay for all AmJobs Programs and Expenses.

    c. <u>Temporary Employees</u> to track their AmJobs "Stipends" and "Training Voucher" payments.

Overview (Continued)

❖ **How does AmJobs Fix Unemployment?**

> **AmJobs will cut Unemployment from 7% to 4% in just two years...and get us back to "Full Employment".**

- In Mid-2013 there were 11.5 Million Unemployed Workers in America. (This represented an Unemployment Rate in the 7% range).
- In order to reach <u>Full Employment</u>, we need to reduce Unemployment to 6 Million Workers (or less).
- Since AmJobs will create 2.9 Million new Jobs every year...in just two years AmJobs will create 5.8 Million New Jobs...reducing unemployment to less than 6 Million Unemployed Workers.

> **Calculation:**

- ✓ (11.5M Unemployed Workers - 5.8M New Jobs = 5.7M "Residual" Unemployed Workers).
- ✓ This represents Full Employment (in the 4% range).

Overview (Continued)

❖ How is AmJobs "Revenue Neutral"?

1. Businesses that join AmJobs will pay only <u>60%</u> of the "average cost of Labor" (for the Temporary Employees they hire) to the State AmJobs Office.
   - ✓ This Payment is called the Businesses "Labor Fee".
   - ✓ It will be paid weekly to the State AmJobs Office.
2. The National average "Median" Hourly Wage is <u>$16.71</u> (Source: Bureau of Labor Statistics).
3. Businesses will pay an average "Labor Fee" of <u>$10.03</u> per hour (60% x $16.71 = $10.03) to the State AmJobs Office...for each Temporary Employee they hire.
4. The State AmJobs Office will use this $10.03 "Labor Fee" per hour (think Revenue Stream) to pay for all AmJobs Expenses...

"Potential" Allocation:

$ 7.50	Worker "Stipends"
$ 1.50	Worker "Training Vouchers"
$ .78	Employment & Training Fund **
$ .12	AmJobs Operating Expenses
$ .12	Miscellaneous & Start-up Costs
$10.03	Total AmJobs costs.

❖ **What is the "Employment and Training Fund"?

This Fund will provide $4.7 Billion in new State Revenue each year... giving each State an average of $94 Million to use for additional "Employment and Training Programs".

Calculations:
- ✓ 2.9M Jobs x $.78 Hourly x 40 hours x 52 weeks = $4.7 Billion.
- ✓ $4.7 Billion / 50 States = $94 Million average per State.

10

Overview (Continued)

❖ **What "Assumptions" were used to create AmJobs?**

> ➤ **AmJobs is based on <u>two</u> "Conservative" Assumptions:**

1. That at least 25% of Unemployed Workers (<u>2.9 Million</u>) will join AmJobs each year, and accept a new Temporary Job.
   - ✓ (25% x 11.5M Unempl. Workers = 2.9 Million workers)

2. That at least 25% of all Businesses in America (<u>1.8 Million</u>) will join AmJobs, and hire an "average" of just <u>two</u> new Temporary Employees each year.
   - ✓ (25% x 7.4M Businesses = 1.8 Million Businesses).

Note: It is likely that most large Businesses will hire dozens (or even hundreds) of new Temporary Workers each year… Making AmJobs even more successful.

❖ **Summary: AmJobs is a "Win/Win" for everyone:**

- <u>Businesses</u> will save up to 40% on new Temporary Labor.
- <u>Unemployed Workers</u> will get a "new Temporary Job" and three valuable Financial Benefits:
    - (1) Keep their "Unemployment Checks"
    - (2) Get weekly "Stipend Payments"…
    - (3) Get weekly "Training Vouchers".
- <u>America</u> will get back to "Full Employment" in just 2 years.
- <u>The Economy</u> will get $60 Billion in new Annual Revenue. (2.9M Jobs x $10.03 per hour x 40 hours x 52 weeks = $60B)

How AmJobs Works
(Next 15 pages)

The next 15 pages will explain the "detailed workings" of the AmJobs Program.

Why I Created AmJobs

(1) Unemployment continues to Plague Our Economy

- For several years, Unemployment has been very high… and only recently has Unemployment inched down below 7%.
- We had 11.5 Million Unemployed Workers in Mid-2013.
- Businesses are not hiring due to "Economic uncertainty" (some Economists believe Businesses are holding over $2 Trillion in cash on the sidelines).
- Millions of Unemployed Workers need "Job Skills Training"… so they can get good jobs and enjoy the "upward mobility" and Benefits of the Middle Class.

(2) "Slow Growth" continues to define our Job Market

- Over the last year, our Economy has been burdened with a "Slow Economic Recovery" … and some Economists predict it will be many years before we get back to "Full Employment".
- AmJobs alone will create 2.9 Million "additional" Temporary Jobs each year (in addition to any normal Job Creation)!

(3) We need a new "Middle Class" Jobs Program that will:

- Create Millions of Temporary Jobs for Unemployed Workers.
- Motivate Businesses to hire Millions of new workers.
- Get us back to "full employment".
- Help our Unemployed Workers learn new "Job Skills"

AmJobs is based on "5 Bold Ideas"

Bold Idea #1

Create <u>Hiring Incentives</u> for Businesses…that will "Save them up to 40% on Labor Costs"… motivate them to Join AmJobs… and Hire 2.9 Million new "Temporary Employees" every year.

Bold Idea #2

Create "<u>Income Incentives</u>" for 2.9 Million Unemployed Workers… that will give them extra Family Income… and motivate them to accept a New "Temporary Job" this year.

Bold Idea #3

Create a "<u>Training Voucher Program</u>" (that will generate $9 Billion each year) to train 2.9 Million Unemployed Workers, allowing them to "go back to school" to learn new "Job Skills".

Bold Idea #4

Create a "<u>State Employment and Training Fund</u>" (that will generate $4.7 Billion each year) so States can Fund new, or expand existing, "Job Creation and Training Programs"… to help all Citizens get better jobs… and learn new "Job Skills".

Bold Idea #5

Provide a "Guarantee" to the American Taxpayer…that AmJobs is 100% Revenue Neutral (will not cost them one dime)!

Note: <u>The next few pages explain these Bold Ideas in "Detail"</u>

Bold Idea #1
(Provide "Hiring Incentives" for Businesses)

AmJobs offers an Irresistible "Hiring Incentive" to Businesses.

❖ Most Businesses have "shovel ready projects" ready to launch:

- But these Projects usually require <u>hiring</u> <u>new</u> <u>employees</u>.
- And when the "Economic future" seems uncertain, Businesses often hold back from hiring.

❖ AmJobs will motivate Businesses to start hiring again, because AmJobs offers a "Hiring Incentive", that allows Businesses to hire New Temporary Employees at only <u>60% of the "normal labor cost"</u>:

- So Businesses will be able to "<u>Save 40%</u>" off the "normal hourly cost" of new labor"!

❖ This 40% Labor Savings is the "KEY" to AmJobs Success!

- It will encourage Businesses to launch new projects.
- It will encourage Businesses to "start hiring again".
- And it will hold down their Costs, and increase their Profits.

❖ The Average "Median" Hourly Wage in America is $16.71.
(Source: Bureau of Labor Statistics).

- Businesses will pay an average "Labor Fee" of <u>$10.03</u> per hour (60% x $16.71 = $10.03) to the State AmJobs Office... for each Temporary Employee they hire.
- They will Save 40% per hour on each Temporary Employee.

Bold Idea #1 (continued)
(Provide "Hiring Incentives" for Businesses)

AmJobs Creates a simple "Two-Step" Flow of Funds Process.

✤ Businesses will not pay Temporary Employees directly.

Rather Businesses will pay their "60% Labor Fees" ($10.03 per hour on average) to the State AmJobs Office (SAO) … and the SAO will use this "60% Labor Fee" to pay Employees their weekly "Stipends" and "Training Vouchers", for each hour they work.

✤ Two-Step Flow of Funds (explained):

1) Businesses will hire Temporary Employees, using the AmJobs "Employment Website" (explained later in detail). Businesses will then calculate each Employee's "60% hourly Rate", using the Employment Website. Businesses will then send their "60% Labor Fees" weekly to the SAO.
   - For Example, if a Business hired a Bookkeeper, whose normal hourly wage was $24.00 per hour, then the Businesses' "60% Labor Fee" would only be $14.40 per hour ($576 for a 40 hour Week).

2) The State AmJobs Office will use this "60% Labor Fee" ($576.00 in above example) to pay for all costs, including: Employee weekly "Stipends", Job Skills "Training Vouchers", contribution to the "Employment and Training Fund", and all AmJobs Administrative expenses.

Note: Temporary Employees will only receive "Payments" from the State AmJobs Office… not from the Businesses they work for.

Bold Idea #1 (continued)
(Provide "Hiring Incentives" for Businesses)

There are certain AmJobs "Rules" that Businesses must follow.

1. AmJobs allows Business to reduce their "labor cost by up to 40%"… But there is a "**Minimum Hourly Threshold**" required:
    - ✓ This "Minimum Hourly Threshold" is $10.03 per hour.
    - ✓ This <u>threshold</u> is needed to ensure "Revenue Neutrality".
    - ✓ Businesses will pay 60% of the "normal hourly labor cost" (or $10.03) whichever is <u>greater</u>…to the AmJobs Office.

2. Businesses will be allowed to increase the size of their workforce by "<u>up to 10%</u>" (or hire 2 new Employees) whichever is <u>greater</u>:
    - ✓ **For Example**: A Business with 80 employees could hire up to 8 additional Temporary Employees (10%)…thus increasing their total workforce to 88 Employees.
    - ✓ But a Small Business with only 10 employees will still be able to hire up to 2 additional Temporary Employees.

3. Businesses can only take advantage of the "60% Labor Incentive" if they hire <u>Additional Employees</u>, increasing the size of their workforce.
    - ✓ Businesses will not be allowed to terminate "Permanent" employees… and replace them with Temporary Employees.

4. The State AmJobs Office will conduct "Audits" to ensure compliance with these "AmJobs Rules".
    - ✓ Any Business that violates these "Rules" will be removed from the AmJobs Program… and they will <u>not be able to Save 40% on Temporary Labor</u>!

17

Bold Idea #1 (continued)
(Provide "Hiring Incentives" for Businesses)

AmJobs also reduces other Business "Employment Risks":

❖ By hiring "Temporary" Employees (rather than "Permanent" Employees) a Business will be reducing some of the risks associated with hiring new employees:

   ✓ If a "Temporary" Employee is not working out (or if the new "Project, Product or Service" is not successful) then the Business can easily eliminate the "Temporary Position", without a lengthy termination process or continuing liability.

AmJobs will help strengthen our Economy by injecting $60 Billion (of new "Spending") into our economy each year:

❖ This $60 Billion represents the total of all "60% Labor Fees" that Businesses send weekly to the State AmJobs Offices (SAO)…to Fund the AmJobs Program.
   (2.9M Workers x $10.03 avg/hour x 40 hours x 52 weeks = $60B)

❖ Then the SAO will use this $60 Billion to pay for all AmJobs Expenses, including:

   ✓ Employee Stipends.
   ✓ Employee Training Vouchers.
   ✓ Payments to the "Employment and Training Fund"… (Allowing more State "Jobs and Training Programs").
   ✓ Operating Expenses (including AmJobs Staff Payroll and Benefits…and any "Miscellaneous or Start-up Costs").

Bold Idea #2
(Provide "Income Incentives" to Unemployed Workers)

AmJobs offers Two important "Income Incentives" to Unemployed Workers...

That will motivate them to Join AmJobs...and accept a new Temporary Job this year:

❖ ***1st Income Incentive:***

     ✓ Most unemployed workers want to go back to work. But they also want to keep the "Unemployment Benefits" they have earned.

     ✓ With AmJobs, Unemployed Workers (who accept a job as a Temporary Employee) will continue to receive their weekly "Unemployment Benefits"... which averaged $300 in 2013.

❖ ***2nd Income Incentive:***

     ✓ AmJobs gives Temporary Employees an "additional" weekly payment (called the AmJobs "Stipend"). This Stipend will equal an "additional" $300 per week (for a 40 hour work week) "doubling" their Family Income.

     ✓ But Temporary Employees will not receive their "AmJobs Stipend" from their new Employer. Rather, they will receive their weekly Stipend directly from the "State AmJobs Office".

Bold Idea #2 (continued)
(Provide "Income Incentives" to Unemployed Workers)

The weekly AmJobs "Stipend" will motivate Unemployed Workers to join AmJobs because this "Stipend" is worth:

* ❖ $300.00 for a <u>40 hour</u> work week.

    * ✓ A Total of $15,600 per year.
    * ✓ ($300.00 x 52 weeks = $15,600 per year)

The weekly "take-home-pay" for every Temporary Employee (that joins AmJobs) will increase significantly.

* ❖ If a worker was receiving $300.00 weekly in "unemployment benefits" (the national average in 2013) and they Joined AmJobs, accepting a Temporary Job (with a 40 hour work week) then their new weekly take-home-pay would "<u>Double</u>":

Weekly Payments	Amount
✓ Unemployment Benefits	$300.00
✓ AmJobs Weekly "Stipend"	<u>$300.00</u>
✓ Total weekly Payments	$600.00

What happens when "Unemployment Benefits" run out?

* ❖ Most employees will continue to work at their new Temporary Job, because they will still earn their $300 weekly "<u>Stipend</u>"...Plus they will also earn Job Skills "Training Vouchers" (which are explained fully in "Bold Idea #3"):

✓ $300 "Stipend"	$300 per week
✓ "Training Vouchers"	<u>$ 60</u> per week
✓ Total Weekly Payments	$360 per week

Bold Idea #2 (continued)
(Provide "Income Incentives" to Unemployed Workers)

AmJobs will help strengthen our Economy by injecting $45 Billion in new "Stipend Spending" each year:

- ❖ This $45 Billion is the total of all "Stipend Payments"…that the State AmJobs Office will pay to Temporary Employees each year.

  ✓ (2.9M Workers x $300 Stipend x 52 weeks = $45B)

AmJobs will provide Jobs to Workers throughout America.

- ❖ Since Businesses are located everywhere…AmJobs will create job opportunities for everyone…everywhere (regardless of: age, gender, sexual orientation, ethnicity, religion, or geographic location (inner-city or rural-countryside).

AmJobs is good for "Labor Unions" too.

- ❖ Under AmJobs, "Union Agreements" will remain exactly the same as they currently are at each Company.
- ❖ If a Company has a Union Agreement…then once a "Temporary Employee" is promoted to a "Permanent Position"…they will join the Union as is customary.
- ❖ Remember, Businesses can only take advantage of AmJobs "40% Labor Savings", if they hire "additional" Employees. (AmJobs forbids Businesses from replacing "Permanent" employees with "Temporary" employees).
- ❖ The AmJobs Office will conduct "Audits" to ensure compliance. Any Businesses violating "AmJobs Rules" will be removed from the Program… losing their 40% labor savings.

Bold Idea #3
(Provide "Training Vouchers" for Unemployed Workers)

> ## AmJobs Offers "Training Vouchers" to Unemployed Workers who join AmJobs and accept a new Temporary Job.

- ❖ AmJobs gives Temporary Employees the opportunity to earn valuable "Training Vouchers" that can be used by them (or their Family) to go back to school to learn New Job Skills.

- ❖ **Each "Training Voucher" is valued at $1.50 per hour:**

   - ✓ These "training vouchers" are worth $60 per week, for a 40 hour work week ($3120 per year).
   - ✓ ($1.50 x 40 hours x 52 weeks = $3120).

> ## All Schools will want to join AmJobs:

   - ✓ AmJobs invites all Schools to join AmJobs, including: Trade Schools, Continuing Education Schools, On-line Schools, Community Colleges, and Universities.

   - ✓ These Schools must agree to accept "Training Vouchers" as payment for "Tuition Costs". Then each School will submit these Vouchers to the State AmJobs Office for reimbursement.

Bold Idea #3 (continued)
(Provide "Training Vouchers" for Unemployed Workers)

Schools will want to join AmJobs for many reasons:

- ❖ <u>More Students:</u> AmJobs will help Schools increase "Student Enrollment" by up to 2.9 Million new Students each year… as Workers use their "Training Vouchers" to register for classes.
- ❖ <u>More Teachers:</u> Schools will hire more Teachers… to meet the needs of these 2.9 Million new Students.
- ❖ <u>More Robust Curriculum:</u> Schools will offer more "Job Skills" Training classes to 2.9 Million new Students each year.
- ❖ <u>More Tuition Revenue:</u> Schools will benefit from an increase in "Revenue"… as 2.9 Million new Students enroll each year.

Note: Each State will determine its own Training Voucher "Value"… based on its own financial needs.

- ❖ The National recommended Voucher Value is <u>$1.50 per hour</u>.
- ❖ But some States may want to "Increase" (or decrease) this value, depending on the amount of "Revenue Generated" in their own State, From the Businesses' "<u>60% Labor Fees</u>".

AmJobs will "Strengthen" our Economy by injecting $9 Billion of new "Training Voucher Spending" each year:

- ❖ This $9 Billion is the total amount of all "Training Vouchers" that the AmJobs Office will send to Temporary Employees. (2.9M Students x $1.50 x 40 hours x 52 weeks = $9 Billion)
- ❖ Temporary Employees (or their Family) will <u>spend</u> these Vouchers on "Job Skills Training"…helping our Economy grow.

Bold Idea #4
(Create the State "Employment and Training Fund")

The State "Employment and Training Fund" can be used by each State to pay for a variety of "Job Creation" and "Job Training" Programs... that will be most valuable to its Citizens.

- ❖ AmJobs will generate $4.7 Billion "Nationally" each year, for States to use for "Employment and Training Programs".

  - ✓ The average amount for each state will be $94 Million.
  - ✓ A State could use this $94 Million to give a $1000 "Educational Grant" to 94,000 Unemployed Workers!

- ❖ Each State will "Collect" their own pro-rata share of this $4.7 Billion...from the "60% Labor Fees" paid by Businesses in their State). They will use these Funds to launch New (or expand existing) Employment and Training Programs.

- ❖ Each State will be able to Fund a variety of State "Job Creation and Training" Programs...that are best for their Citizens...like:

  - ✓ Apprenticeship Programs.
  - ✓ Financial Aid (Grants) for "Job Skills Training".
  - ✓ More "One-Stop Career Centers" services.
  - ✓ Expansion of "The Jobs Corps".
  - ✓ Senior (or Youth) "Job Skills" Training Programs.
  - ✓ Veterans Re-employment Programs.
  - ✓ Minority "Jobs or Training" Programs.
  - ✓ Disabled Worker "Rehabilitation and Job Training... etc.

Bold Idea #4 (continued)
(Create the State "Employment and Training Fund")

The "Employment and Training Fund" will help Workers believe again in the "American Dream"... that they can:

- ✓ Get a good Job...
- ✓ Raise a family...
- ✓ Own a home...
- ✓ And Save for a comfortable retirement.

❖ Each State can determine its own "Employment and Training Fund" <u>Value</u>, based on its own Financial Needs.

❖ **The recommended "National Contribution Target" for the <u>Employment and Training Fund</u> is $.78 per hour.**

❖ But some States may want to "Increase" (or decrease) this value, depending upon the amount of <u>Revenue generated</u> in their State, from the "60% Labor Fees" from Businesses.

❖ <u>AmJobs allows flexibility</u>, so each State can design its own customized "Employment and Training Fund"... in order to maximize Citizen Benefits, while <u>staying within its Budget</u>.

AmJobs will Strengthen our Economy by injecting $4.7 Billion in "Employment and Training Revenue" to the States yearly:

➢ This $4.7 Billion is the total amount of "contributions" that each State AmJobs Office will generate for their State:
(2.9M Workers x $0.78 Contribution x 40 hours x 52 weeks = $4.7B)

Bold Idea #5
(Provide a "Guarantee" to the American Taxpayer)

AmJobs will not cost the American Taxpayer "one dime"!

> The "60% Labor Fees" from Businesses...that are sent weekly to the State AmJobs Offices (SAO)... will pay for 100% of all AmJobs Costs.

All AmJobs Costs are "100% funded", including:

* ❖ The weekly "AmJobs Stipends" to Temporary Employees.
* ❖ The "Job Skills Training Vouchers" Program.
* ❖ Funding for the AmJobs "Employment and Training Fund".
* ❖ All SAO operating costs (i.e. Payroll, Benefits and Overhead).
* ❖ All Miscellaneous costs (including AmJobs "start up costs").

AmJobs generates ample Revenue to pay for all Costs...Including "Start-up Costs":

* ❖ At the beginning of AmJobs, there will be a few start-up costs, including creating the "Employment Website".
* ❖ These "start up costs" will be "fully reimbursed" by the AmJobs Program...from the "60% Business Labor Fees".
* ❖ Even if the "AmJobs Website Development" costs are $380 Million (the estimate for the "Affordable Care Act" Website) ...the reimbursement will be completed in just 6.2 months...with Payments from the "Miscellaneous Budget":
  ($380M cost / $61M "Monthly Misc Budget" = 6.2 Months)

How Will AmJobs Create "2.9 Million" New Jobs Every Year?

AmJobs is based on Two "Very Conservative Assumptions":

❖ *Conservative Assumption #1*:

At least "25%" of America's 11.5 Million Unemployed Workers will join AmJobs each year... and accept a New Temporary Job.

- ✓ These Workers will need 2.9 Million New Jobs each year.
- ✓ (25% x 11.5M Unemployed Workers = 2,875,000 Jobs)

❖ *Conservative Assumption #2:*

At least "25%" of America's 7,354,000 Businesses (Source: BLS) will Join AmJobs, and hire an "average" of two New Employees.

- ✓ Of course many "Large Business" will hire dozens (or even hundreds) of New Temporary Employees each year.
- ✓ And many "Small Businesses" will hire more than just "one".
- ✓ So Businesses will have the ability to create 3.7 Million Jobs.
- ✓ (25% x 7,354,000 Businesses x 2 Employees = 3,677,000 Jobs).

❖ **Note:** AmJobs only needs 2.9 Million new Temporary Jobs (not the 3.7 Million new Jobs that Businesses can create)... So AmJobs will easily provide all the new Temporary Jobs needed.

These "conservative assumptions" probably understate the actual number of new Jobs that will be created!

- ✓ It is possible that 30% to 40% of all "Unemployed Workers" and Businesses will Join AmJobs...so the actual number of new Jobs created could be much greater!

Government Participation in AmJobs
(Next 4 pages)

The next 4 pages will describe how the Federal and State Governments will "manage" the AmJobs Program.

"Federal" AmJobs Office Responsibilities

❖ **The "Federal" AmJobs Office has <u>two</u> major responsibilities:**

(1) <u>Develop "Standardized Procedures"</u> (Templates) that the States can use to create their own "AmJobs Program".

(2) <u>Perform "Advisory Services"</u> for the States… to help them develop "best practices" and "management processes".

Note: The Federal AmJobs Office will be reimbursed by the States (from the "60% Labor Fees") for all costs incurred.

❖ **Here is a list of the "Standardized" Guides and Templates to be developed by the "Federal" AmJobs Office:**

- **A "National AmJobs Guide"**, that the States can use to develop their own individual **State** AmJobs Program.
- **An "AmJobs Employment Website"** that the States can use as a "template" to develop their own "Employment Website" (so they can facilitate all State AmJobs Operating Procedures).
- **A "60% Wage Rate List" Template**, that States can use to develop their own "60% Wage Rate List" (so Businesses can calculate the weekly "60% Labor Fees" owed to the State AmJobs Office).
- **A "Training Voucher" Guide,** that the States can use to develop their own "Training Voucher Program".
- **An "Employment and Training Fund" Guide,** that the States can use to develop their own "Employment and Training Fund".
- **"Marketing Communications" Templates**, including: Brochures, Press Releases, Staff Training Manuals, etc… that will help the States develop their own "AmJobs Communication Programs".
- **An "Oversight and Compliance" Guide**, that the States can use to create "best practices" for **Business Audits** (to ensure Compliance with AmJobs Rules and Requirements).

"State" AmJobs Office Responsibilities

Each State AmJobs Office (SAO) will be responsible for:

1. The creation of its "Employment Website"... to "mirror" the National Website Template. This will allow:

- ✓ Businesses to post available Jobs.
- ✓ Workers to "post resumes"...and apply for jobs.
- ✓ Businesses to enter "new employee information".
- ✓ Businesses to enter "weekly employee hours worked".
- ✓ Businesses to Calculate their "60% Labor Fees"... that they will send to the SAO each week.
- ✓ The SAO to track all "60% Labor Fees" from Businesses ...and use Collection Procedures if necessary.
- ✓ The SAO to print the weekly "Stipend Payments" and "Training Vouchers"...to be mailed out to Employees.
- ✓ The SAO to calculate Transfer Payments, to be deposited into the State "Employment and Training Fund".
- ✓ Employees to view and track their "hours worked", "Stipend Payments" and "Training Vouchers".
- ✓ Schools to get reimbursed (by the SAO) for "Training Vouchers" accepted for Tuition Payments.
- ✓ The SAO to create "Reports" to help it Manage AmJobs, conduct audits, and ensure compliance.

Note: Access to various "Website Sections" will be granted to Businesses, Temporary Employees, Schools, and the SAO via "security passwords" ...to ensure the privacy and security of data.

2. The creation of the State's "60% Wage Rate List"… Showing the "60% Hourly Wage" for each Job Classification:

❖ Businesses will use this List, to calculate the "60% Labor Fees" to pay the State AmJobs Office. (A Bookkeeper's Job Classification might be $24.00 per hour…so the 60% listing would be $14.40).

3. The "Collection and Disbursement" of all AmJobs Revenue. Businesses will pay their "60% Labor Fees", based on number of "Hours Worked" by each AmJobs Temporary Employee they hire:

❖ The National Average "60% Labor Fee", that Businesses will pay to AmJobs is $10.03 per hour:
($16.71 Average "Median" Wage x 60% = $10.03)

❖ The National "Revenue Allocation Per Hour" might be:
✓	"Stipend Payments"	$7.50
✓	"Training Vouchers"	$1.50
✓	"Employment & Training Fund" contribution	$0.78
✓	AmJobs Office "Operating Expenses"	$0.12
✓	Miscellaneous and Start-up Costs	$0.12
✓	National Hourly Cost (after rounding)	$10.03

4. The handling of all Communications … including: Public Relations, Media Relations, Government Relations, etc.

5. Providing Liaison Services between: Businesses, Workers, Schools and Government (with problem resolution provided if needed).

6. Providing "Oversight and Compliance" … by creating "best practices"… and conducting "Business Audits" to ensure compliance.

AmJobs Implementation Process
(Time Line)

The "Launch of AmJobs" will require each State to complete <u>Three Major Tasks</u>:

1. <u>Design of the Employment "Website"</u> (3 to 6 months)

- Hire a Software Company to "mirror" the National Website
- <u>Fully</u> <u>Test</u> the Website before launch...to ensure it performs properly...and is ready to "Serve all AmJobs Stakeholders".

2. <u>Education of the Citizens of each State</u>. (3 to 6 months)

- <u>Create all AmJobs "Communications Materials"</u> to explain AmJobs to all AmJobs Stakeholders...For example:
    - ✓ An "Information Website" (How to use AmJobs).
    - ✓ Brochures and "CD-Tutorials".
    - ✓ Local Seminars.
    - ✓ "You-Tube Videos"...etc.

- **<u>Develop "Speakers Notes"</u>** for Political Leaders to use in their "Media Presentations"...to promote AmJobs.

3. <u>Hire and Train the State's AmJobs Staff</u> (3 to 6 months)

- The "Administrative Staff" of each State AmJobs Office must be "hired and trained".
- The Staff must be prepared to provide "knowledgeable Customer Support" to all AmJobs Stakeholders, including: Businesses, Workers, Schools, and Government Offices.

"Quick Review" of AmJobs
(Next 2 pages)

The next 2 pages will review why all
"Stakeholders" will support AmJobs.

AmJobs "Quick Review"

❖ "Businesses" will Join AmJobs because they will:

- "Save" up to 40% on Labor Costs… for new Temporary Employees they hire.
- **Note**: There is a "Minimum Hourly Threshold" (of $10.03 per hour) that Businesses must pay for each new Employee. This "Threshold" ensures that AmJobs is "100% Revenue Neutral".

❖ "Unemployed Workers" will Join because they will:

1. Keep their "unemployment checks" while working at their new Job (they will not lose any benefits).
2. Receive AmJobs "Stipends" worth $300 per week (for a 40 hour work week)…which equals $15,600 per year.
3. Receive valuable "Training Vouchers" worth $60 per week…$3120 per year. This will allow them (or their family) to go back to School to learn valuable new "Job Skills".

Value of Worker Benefits	40 Hour Week	Annual
Keep Unemployment Checks	$300.00*	$15,600
AmJobs Stipend	$300.00	$15,600
Training Voucher Payments	$ 60.00	$ 3120
Total Value of Benefits	$660.00	$34,320

* **Note**: $300.00 was the average weekly "Unemployment Benefit" paid in 2013 (Source: Center for Budget Policies & Priorities).

AmJobs "Quick Review"
(Continued)

❖ **Schools will support AmJobs because they will:**

- Get up to 2.9 Million new Students each year.
- Increase their Tuition Revenue and Profits.

❖ **States will support AmJobs because they will:**

- Reduce their "Unemployment Rate" significantly.
- Provide "Training Benefits" for Unemployed Workers.
- Receive Funds for their <u>Employment and Training Fund</u>, which will pay for more "Job Creation and Training" Programs.
- Reduce their "Unemployment Insurance Costs" (over time) … as Workers gain new Job Skills, get new jobs, and begin to pay Unemployment Insurance Taxes again.

❖ **"Taxpayers" will Support AmJobs because:**

- AmJobs will "fix our Unemployment Problem"… and get America back to "Full Employment" in just 2 years.
- AmJobs will help our Citizens gain new Jobs Skills… so they can get better Jobs in the future.
- AmJobs will help our Economy Grow.
- AmJobs will <u>not</u> cost the Taxpayer one dime!

❖ **The Economy will Benefit from AmJobs because:**

- AmJobs will inject <u>$60 Billion</u> of "New Revenue" into our Economy each year… Helping Businesses become more profitable, Workers prosper, and our Economy Grow.

"Hypothetical" State AmJobs Programs
(Next 3 pages)

> **The next 3 pages will explain how two <u>State</u> AmJobs Programs "might" be created:**
>
> **(<u>Florida</u> and <u>New Jersey</u> are used as examples)**

Each State will "modify" AmJobs as Needed

Each State will use the National AmJobs <u>Templates</u> and <u>Guides</u>...to help it design its "own unique" AmJobs Program.

- ❖ **<u>Each State AmJobs Program will be "Similar"</u>** (but not "Identical").

- ❖ **<u>Each State will develop its own "State AmJobs Office",</u>** and hire and train its own AmJobs Staff. (It will use the <u>National</u> "Employee Hiring and Training Template" as a guide).

- ❖ **<u>Each State will design its own "Employment Website"</u>** that will support all "AmJobs Operating Processes". (It will use the "<u>National</u> Employment Website Template" as a guide).

- ❖ **<u>Each State will develop its own unique AmJobs "Budget":</u>**

  - ✓ Each State will have a <u>unique</u> combination of "Unemployed Workers" and "Median" Hourly Wage.
  - ✓ Consequently, each State's will have a unique "Revenue Stream" (Revenue per Hour) ... that it collects from the "60% Labor Fees" from Businesses.
  - ✓ The <u>National</u> Average "Revenue per Hour" (received from Businesses Labor Fees) will be $10.03 per hour.
  - ✓ But the actual "Revenue per Hour" (received by each State from Businesses) may be "Higher or Lower" that this average.

- ❖ **<u>On the next 2 pages Florida and New Jersey are used as Examples</u>**... to demonstrate how each State's "Revenue per Hour" might be "<u>Higher</u> or <u>Lower</u>" than the "National Average".

Florida -- Example #1
(A "Hypothetical" State AmJobs Program)

❖ **In Mid-2013, Florida had an unemployment rate near 7%**... with about 665,300 Unemployed Workers. But Florida can <u>Fix</u> its Unemployment Problem by creating the <u>Florida AmJobs Program</u>.

  ✓ Florida can use the National AmJobs "Templates" and "Guides" to create the <u>Florida AmJobs Program</u>.

  ✓ Florida will allow Businesses to hire Temporary Employees at <u>60% of the normal "Hourly Wage"</u> for each Job Classification.

  ✓ Florida's "Median" Hourly Wage was $14.72 (source: B.L.S.)

  ✓ There will be a "Minimum Hourly <u>Threshold</u>" of $8.83 per hour, which Businesses must pay, to ensure that AmJobs is "Revenue Neutral".
    (60% x $14.72 = $8.83).

  ✓ Florida will create its own "Training Voucher Program" and "Employment and Training Fund"… and the Funding for each will be derived from the "AmJobs Revenue Stream" that Florida collects from the Businesses' "60% Labor Fees".

❖ **Since Florida is unique, its "Hourly Revenue Allocation" may be slightly <u>Lower</u> than the "National" Hourly Revenue Allocation:**

"Hypothetical" Allocation:	"National" Hourly Allocation	"Florida" Hourly Allocation
▪ AmJobs Stipend	$7.50	$7.50
▪ Training Vouchers	$1.50	$1.00
▪ Employment and Training Fund	$0.78	$0.09
▪ Administrative Costs	$ 0.12	$0.12
▪ Misc & "Start-up Costs"	$ 0.12	$0.12
▪ Total Hourly Allocation	$10.03	$ 8.83

New Jersey -- Example #2
(A "Hypothetical" State AmJobs Program)

❖ **In Mid-2013, New Jersey had an unemployment rate over 8%...**
with about 394,600 Unemployed Workers. But New Jersey can <u>Fix</u>
its Unemployment Problem, by creating the "<u>NJ AmJobs Program</u>."

   ✓ New Jersey can use the National AmJobs
   "Templates" and "Guides" to create the New Jersey
   AmJobs Program.

   ✓ NJ will allow Businesses to hire Temporary
   Employees at <u>60% of the normal "Hourly Wage"</u> for
   each Job Classification.

   ✓ NJ's "Median" Hourly Wage was $19.17 (Source: B.L.S.)

   ✓ There will be a "Minimum Hourly Threshold" of
   $11.50 per hour, which Businesses must pay, to
   ensure that AmJobs is "Revenue Neutral".
   (60% x $19.17 = $11.50).

   ✓ New Jersey will create its own "Training Voucher
   Program" and "Employment and Training Fund", and
   the Funding for each will be derived from the "AmJobs
   Revenue Stream" that New Jersey collects from the
   Businesses'"60% Labor Fees".

❖ **Since New Jersey is <u>unique</u>, its "Hourly Revenue
Allocation" may be slightly <u>Higher</u> than the "National"
Hourly Revenue Allocation:**

"Hypothetical" Allocation:	National Hourly Allocation	New Jersey Hourly Allocation
■ AmJobs Stipend	$7.50	$7.50
■ Training Vouchers	$1.50	$1.75
■ Employment and Training Fund	$0.78	$2.01
■ Administrative Costs	$ 0.12	$0.12
■ Misc & "Start-up Costs"	$ 0.12	$0.12
■ Total Hourly Allocation	$10.03	$11.50

Financial Appendices
(Next 3 pages)

The next 3 pages will provide some "financial details" supporting the AmJobs Program.

Appendices:

1. <u>National</u> Financial "Summary"

2. <u>Florida</u> Financial "Summary"

3. <u>New Jersey</u> Financial "Summary"

Note: All Statistics used in this Booklet come from the following Sources:

- ✓ Bureau of Labor Statistics
- ✓ US Census Bureau
- ✓ Center for Budget Policies & Priorities

Appendix #1
"National" Financial (Summary)

❖ **Potential Number of new "National" Temporary Jobs**, that could be Created each year, if only 25% of Businesses join AmJobs, and hire an average of just "two" Workers: ___*3.7 Million*___

❖ **Number of Unemployed Workers**, who will "Accept" a new Temporary Job, if only 25% join AmJobs each year: ___*2.9 Million*___

❖ **Estimated AmJobs "Annual Revenue Stream"** (60% Labor Fees) paid by Businesses to the AmJobs Office: ___*$60 Billion*___

❖ **Estimated AmJobs Expense Allocation:**	**Expenses (in Billions)**	**% Revenue Allocation**
■ Weekly "Stipend Pay" to Temp. Employees:	$44.9 B	74.8%
■ "Training Vouchers" paid to Temp Employees:	$ 9.0 B	15.0%
■ "Employment and Training Fund" Contribution	$ 4.7 B	7.8%
■ AmJobs Administrative Office costs:	$ 0.7 B	1.2%
■ Miscellaneous & "Start-up" Costs:	$ 0.7 B	1.2%
■ Total Annual AmJobs Expenses	$60 Billion	100%

❖ **AmJobs is 100% Revenue Neutral**:
- ✓ AmJobs will generate $60 Billion in "Revenue" each year.
- ✓ The estimated Operating Expenses are also $60 Billion per year.
- ✓ AmJobs pays for itself every year.
- ✓ AmJobs will <u>not</u> cost the American Taxpayer one dime!

Note: If you would like Complete Financial "Details and Calculations"… just contact us… and we will provide them.

Appendix #2
"Florida" AmJobs Financial Summary

❖ **Potential Number of new "Florida" Temporary Jobs**, that could be Created each year, if only 25% of Businesses join AmJobs, and hire an average of just "two" Workers: ***245,400***

❖ **Number of "Florida" Unemployed Workers**, who will "Accept" a new Temporary Job, if only 25% join AmJobs each year: ***166,300***

❖ **Estimated AmJobs "Annual Revenue Stream"** (60% Labor Fees) paid by Businesses to the AmJobs Office: ***$3.1 Billion***

❖ **Estimated AmJobs Expense Allocation:**	**Expenses** (B=Billions) (M=Millions)	**% of Revenue Allocation**
▪ Weekly "Stipend Pay" to Temp. Employees	$ 2.6 B	84.9%
▪ "Training Vouchers" paid to Temp Employees	$346 M	11.3%
▪ "Employment and Training Fund" Contribution	$ 32 M	1.0%
▪ AmJobs Administrative Office costs:	$ 42 M	1.4%
▪ Miscellaneous & Start-up Costs:	$ 42 M	1.4%
▪ Total Annual Florida AmJobs Expenses	$3.1 Billion	100%

❖ **The Florida AmJobs Program is 100% Revenue Neutral**...
- AmJobs will generate $3.1 Billion in "Florida Revenue" each year.
- The estimated Operating Expenses are also $3.1 Billion.
- AmJobs pays for itself every year.
- AmJobs will <u>not</u> cost the Florida Taxpayer one dime!

Note: If you would like Complete Financial "Details and Calculations"... just contact us... and we will provide them.

Appendix-3
"New Jersey" AmJobs Financial (Summary)

❖ **Potential Number of new "New Jersey" Temporary Jobs**, that could be Created each year, if only 25% of Businesses join AmJobs, and hire an average of just two Workers: **_113,400_**

❖ **Number of N.J. Unemployed Workers**, who will "Accept" a new Temporary Job, if only 25% join AmJobs each year: **_98,650_**

❖ **Estimated AmJobs "Annual Revenue Stream**" (60% Labor Fees) paid by Businesses to the AmJobs Office: **_$2.4 Billion_**

❖ **Estimated AmJobs Expense Allocation:**	**Expenses (B=Billions) (M=Millions)**	**% of Revenue Allocation**
▪ Weekly "Stipend Pay" to Temp. Employees:	$ 1.54 B	65.2%
▪ "Training Vouchers" paid to Temp Employees:	$359 M	15.2%
▪ "Employment and Training Fund" Contribution:	$413 M	17.5%
▪ AmJobs Administrative Office costs:	$ 25 M	1.0%
▪ Miscellaneous & Start-up Costs:	$ 25 M	1.0%
▪ Total Annual NJ AmJobs Expenses	$2.4 Billion	100%

❖ **The New Jersey AmJobs Program is 100% Revenue Neutral**...
  - ▪ AmJobs will generate $2.4 Billion in "NJ Revenue" each year.
  - ▪ The estimated NJ Operating Expenses are also $2.4 Billion.
  - ▪ AmJobs pays for itself every year.
  - ▪ AmJobs will <u>not</u> cost the New Jersey Taxpayer one dime!

Note: If you would like Complete Financial "Details and Calculations"... just contact us... and we will provide them.

Rocky Lynn
Founder and Chairman
AmJobs (The American Jobs Program)

Rocky Lynn is a retired Telesales Executive from
New Jersey, now living in Florida, who devotes
his time to helping Unemployed Americans "get
back to work"... and upgrade their "Job Skills."

As the Founder of AmJobs (The American Jobs Program) Rocky has
developed an innovative Jobs Program, that will create 2.9 Million new
Temporary Jobs every year. This will reduce America's Unemployment
Rate from 7% to 4% in just two years. At the same time, AmJobs will
provide "Job Skills Training" for 2.9 Million Unemployed Workers every
year. AmJobs is 100% Revenue Neutral ... and will inject $60 Billion into
our Economy each year. You can Visit AmJobs Online at: AmJobs.org

From 1991 to 2007, Rocky was a Director of Telesales for Verizon
Wireless. He was responsible for several "Sales Call Centers", with
350 Sales and Support Representatives, plus Supervisors and
Managers. Call Center Sales of Wireless Phones, Accessories, and
Data Services exceeded 500,000 per year.

Prior to joining Verizon Wireless, Rocky was the President and CEO
of Radio & TV Registry, Ltd. He owned and managed two "Sales Call
Centers" in NYC, with 125 Sales and Support Representatives, plus
Supervisors and Managers. The Company provided specialized
Telemarketing Services to Companies, including: Television Advertising
Response, Order Processing, and "Bilingual" Hispanic Telesales.

Rocky was an Officer in the United States Air Force. As a Captain
and Titan 2 Missile Crew Commander, Rocky was Responsible for
the Nuclear Missile, the ten story underground launch silo, and
his Missile Combat Crew.

Rocky is an Economics and Finance Graduate from the University
of Denver, where he received his BS and MBA Degrees.